Stremmel House

THE MONACELLI PRESS

Stremmel House

Mark Mack

Introduction by Mark Mack · Afterword by Peter Stremmel

Photographs by Richard Barnes

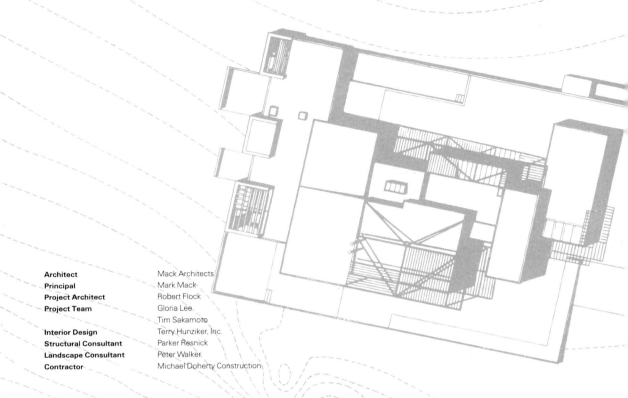

Architect	Mack Architects
Principal	Mark Mack
Project Architect	Robert Flock
Project Team	Gloria Lee
	Tim Sakamoto
Interior Design	Terry Hunziker, Inc.
Structural Consultant	Parker Resnick
Landscape Consultant	Peter Walker
Contractor	Michael Doherty Construction

First published in the United States of America in 1998 by
The Monacelli Press, Inc.,
10 East 92nd Street, New York, New York 10128.

Library of Congress Cataloging-in-Publication Data
Stremmel House : Mark Mack / introduction by Mark Mack ;
afterword by Peter Stremmel ; photographs by Richard Barnes.
p. cm.—(One house)
ISBN 1-885254-49-0
1. Stremmel House (Reno, Nev.). 2. Color in architecture—Nevada—Reno. 3. Architecture,
Modern—20th century—Nevada—Reno. 4. Reno (Nev.)—Buildings, structures, etc.
5. Mack, Mark—Criticism and interpretation. I. Mack, Mark. II. Series.
NA7238.R46S76 1997
728'.37'0979355—dc21   97-39001

Printed and bound in Italy

Designed and composed by *Group* C Inc. New Haven/Boston

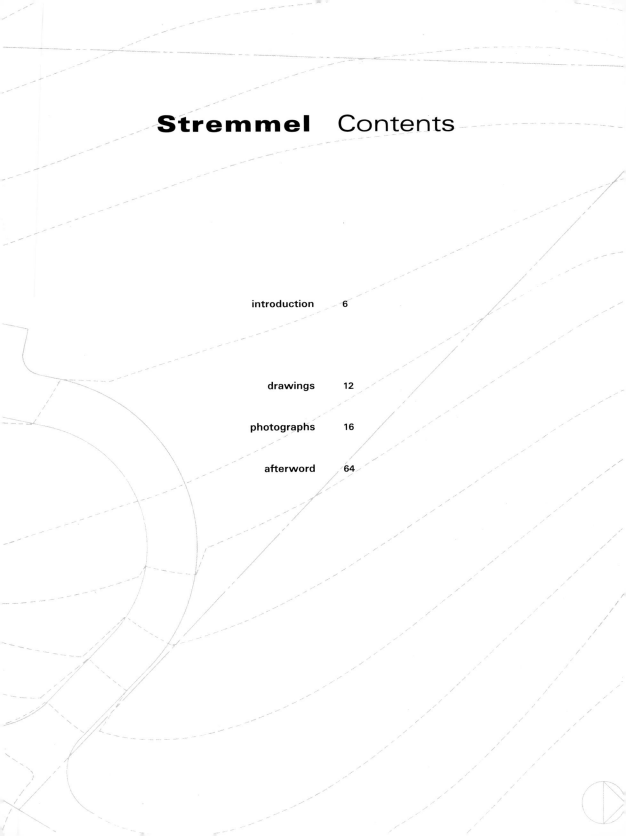

Stremmel Contents

Introduction
Mark Mack

I was coming off the typical Californian experience of skiing in the sunny Sierras when I first met Peter and Turkey Stremmel. I remember coming down the mountain into Reno, a harsh, desert climate with an architectural environment of pseudo-adobe styles varying only in degrees of pretension, and arriving at their new lot to find myself in an almost surreal, scaleless landscape of sagebrush and wildflowers. In the distance were the twin cities of Reno and Sparks with their arid cityscapes and sporadically planned, large-scale hotels and casinos. Occasional airplanes approaching Reno/Tahoe International Airport were at eye level.

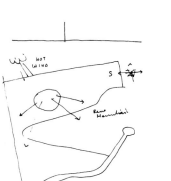

Pete wanted me to see the site first, before I saw how he and Turkey lived, because they had outlived their adobe of southwestern persuasion. They wanted instead a large yet comfortable house, one that complemented their art gallery job/lifestyle. I felt their house should be an extension of their work—displaying, collecting, and living with art. I told them architecture is not a piece of art; it is more or less an artful arrangement of many concerns—a compromise of ideas that uses construction as a vessel for beautiful spatial and practical possibilities.

We walked around the site with our backs to the west, where Pete said the strong afternoon winds would come from. The large boulders on the site suggested a point of anchoring—a kind of definition that would allow you to feel a kinship to the wide open land. As the sun started to go down over the western Sierras, the wind picked up, and the lights in Reno began to flicker at twilight. It was time to catch my flight home to Los Angeles. Just before we left, we walked around the perimeter of the eight-acre site to make sure that the place where we had first set foot was the place to build the house.

The Concept: Shed, Boundaries, Domestic Bliss

Shed   One of my first trips into the California desert and the High Sierra was in search of hot springs with several friends from New York and San Francisco. Traveling the highways we encountered sheds made of wood posts and corrugated metal, which were used to shade equipment, hay, or livestock. The simplicity of these four-post structures in the rural desert landscape recalled a drawing by Walter Pichler, an Austrian artist. This drawing

depicts a figure lying under a small shed, which is large enough to cover only his head, leaving his torso and feet exposed. The title, I remembered vaguely, involved the memory of a tree house the artist had built as a child. This image of the sheltered mind and the unsheltered body appears practical on one level and yet incomplete on another, suggesting a conflict between memory and reality, necessity and emotion. These images and concepts triggered my thoughts for designing the Stremmel House.

Boundaries   Among the more startling differences to me in the western part of the United States was how boundaries of states, districts, and lots were configured. The further west you move, the more gridlike, the more regular, the borders and boundaries become. These boundaries are determined by geometry rather than by the layering of division, arbitrariness, conflict, and geographic landscape features—as found in Europe and even the eastern United States. This phenomenon, echoing the simplicity and naïveté of the West, was reflected in the Stremmel site, a subdivision divided only by the irregularity of the access street, which carved its way between rock formations. This kind of geometric division became the basis for the layout of the site, the rooms, and the walls.

Domestic Bliss   The house is large not only in two dimensions; it is also tall. Yet it is essentially a one-story building with an occasional second level. In the almost scaleless dimension of the high desert, the house had to relate to both the outer landscape and the inner domestic landscape of furniture and household equipment. Another challenge was to accommodate large artworks and create comfortable spaces at a large scale. There were very few restrictions in terms of program and budget, so I needed to define the parameters of the house in terms of my own limitations and desires. This freedom reminds me of Adolf Loos when he writes:

The work of art is revolutionary; the house is conservative. The work of art shows people new directions and thinks of the future. The house thinks of the present. Man loves everything that satisfies his comfort. He hates everything that wants to take him out of his acquired and secured position and that disturbs him. Thus he loves the house and hates art. Does it follow that the house has nothing in common with art and is architecture not to be included amongst the arts? That is so. Only a small part of architecture belongs to art: the tomb and the monument. Everything else that fulfils a function is to be excluded from the domain of art. "Architektur" (1910)

Trellis, Plinth, House, and Colors

Trellis   The harsh sun and the uncompromising surroundings required more than just a conventional house as domestic shelter. I envisioned early on the idea of a shed covering the house to create a large mediating envelope for living and to allow year-round use of the outdoor spaces. This concept developed into a trellis structure integrated into the house that would serve as a unifying element, mediate the indoor/outdoor spaces, and provide a transition of scale between the various parts of the house.

Plinth   Laid out like a geometer's rectangle, the shape of the plinth represents the taming of the landscape by humans. Cutting into the slightly sloping landscape, the plinth is the demarcation between the domestic and natural landscapes. Also, due to ecological concerns for the fragility of the high desert landscape (sagebrush, wildflowers, and blooming moss need years to recover from destruction), the plinth was built as the boundary for all construction activities. To the west and north, the plinth is recessed into the land, creating a wall that protects from the wind and the occasional wild animal; to the east and the south, it is an elevated platform that offers a view of the landscape. The plinth also reinforces the concept of private and public by enclosing the backyard with its lap pool and

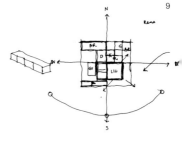

informal domestic landscape while accenting the formal qualities of the front-yard reflecting pool and lawn.

House The rooms are organized by their functional dependencies and spatial requirements, which resulted in a dual yet distinct relationship between the private and public dimensions. This is evident in the informal approach from the garages to the family room to the kitchen to the bedrooms as well as in the formal approach from the entry to the living room to the dining room. The trellis construction and scale reflect these two paths. It starts high (about twenty-eight feet) as a gesture to the formal entry and slopes down toward the living room, where it transforms into a solid roof covering the dining room and emerges again as an open trellis in front of the kitchen and the family room. It terminates at a low point (about ten feet) where the dogs sleep.

The rooms follow the same path: the formal entry sequence opens up to the towering living room—a place to live around and display large artworks. The loftlike library, overlooking the living room, offers a cozy retreat within the towering space. The kitchen, echoing the formal/informal relationship, faces both the dining room and family room and is separated by ceiling-high sliding doors. The bedrooms are grouped together along a lower part of the house. They are intentionally separated in one sense and yet visually connected with the house and the ground. The bedrooms endure the extremes of sun, snow, and wind, and each one has a covered exterior space in front of it that acts as a shelter and buffer between the rooms and the desert. The large study serves as the transition from the living room to the more private area of the bedrooms and looks out over the desert landscape.

Colors The materials and colors of the house reflect the functions of each component. The guest room is a large space with a living area on the ground floor and a loftlike sleeping area above. Its L-shaped yellow form (I associate the color yellow with openness and optimism) frames the entry and represents a visual gate to the house. To the side, in the

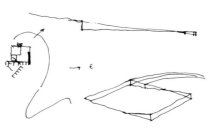

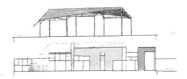

low garage enclosure, is a wall guiding you through the entry door into the two-story living room at the center of the house. The living room, a large, light-filled stucco box, is a burnt earthy-orange color to complement the yellow of the domestic structures. All other parts of the building associated with service functions—the garage, bathrooms, mechanical rooms, hallways, and landscape features—are made of two shades of purple/gray ground-face concrete block. This further differentiates the functional aspects of the building. The breezeway, roof, and ceiling of the dining room are articulated in common materials. Most prominent are corrugated metal sheets, reminiscent of the utilitarian structures found in agricultural communities, arranged to express the more industrial character of the shed. In the bedroom wing, the shade structures that protrude over the stone walls are again of yellow stucco, in order to address the connection to the land by mimicking the boulders in the desert landscape.

The materials and their respective colors establish subtle distinctions or unions between public and private, formal and informal, inside and outside. The cool and warm colors of the plaster walls reflect the public/private atmospheres for living and viewing art. In the kitchen, stained ash cabinets in tones of cherry and yellow accentuate the duality of formal and informal: the cabinets facing the formal dining room are in dark hues and those facing the informal dining room are lighter. Finally, the articulation of concrete floors, stained in gray, terra-cotta, and warm brown, visually unite different spaces with continuous planes. Similarly, the exposed metal ceiling of the dining room extends outside, weaving together interior and exterior.

Easy Living

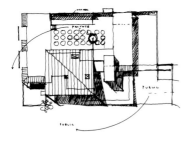

The Stremmel House is, to me, my most "Californian" house. Although it is in Nevada, it incorporates many of the ideals of house and home that I have tried to develop since arriving in California in 1975. I have never conceived houses as objects by themselves, and the Stremmel House is no exception. It avoids the temptation to be placed in the landscape as an *objet d'art.* "Easy living" is the virtue and openness is the strategy.

The open circular plan, which oscillates between formal and informal spaces, eases circulation through the house and avoids corridors and single-function spaces in order to promote multivalent spaces of domesticity and informality. All rooms are connected to the outside with large operational openings, such as sliding and pivoting doors, and open onto patios, terraces, and decks. This connection to the outdoors is reinforced by the extension of the concrete floors to the outside where a fireplace conditions the exterior spaces.

The trellis represents the "in-between" space—the space between inside and outside; it formalizes the use of the outdoor spaces. It creates spaces ideal for the climatic conditions of California. In this house, the trellis, from the tall front to the low back, mediates between the public and private spaces of the house.

In all the houses I have built in California, there is a clear distinction between what is public (formal) and what is private (informal). This split—and the recognition of it—is a holdover from European tradition, where the distinction is evident in almost all aspects of life and culture. The trellis, the plinth, the tall and shorter structures, the pool, and the domestic garden, as well as the reflective moat, express notions associated with the play between formal and informal.

I associate California with color. Color is present in all aspects of Californian culture, reflecting a culture that does not see relationships as opposites—black and white, truth and lie— or as dogmatic gospel. The emotional aspect of color, especially in domestic architecture, where it deals with individuals and their preferences, is to me a testimonial to nonconformity and individuality. It is an aspect fully developed on the West Coast and typifies the concept of "easy living." This contrasts starkly with the so-called refinement of the European tradition, which shows its colors only in the vernacular and "homey" articulations of "low" culture.

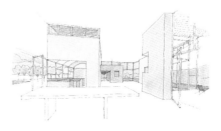

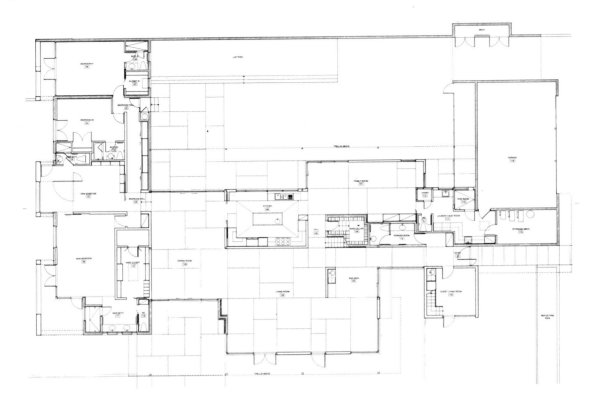

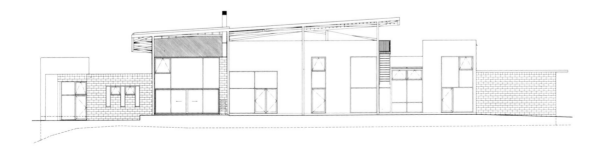

first floor plan; front (east) elevation

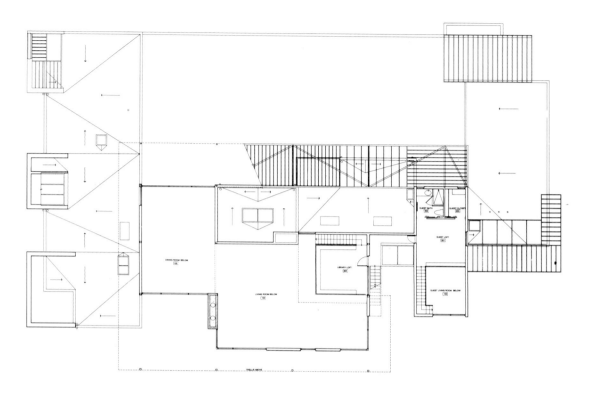

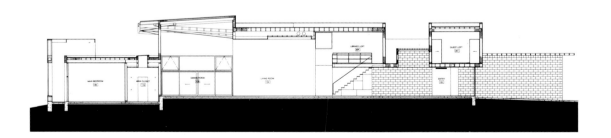

mezzanine plan; longitudinal section

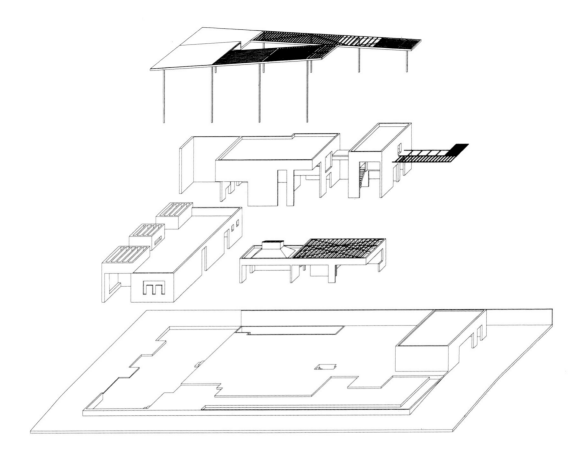

axonometric showing separate elements; rendering of east facade

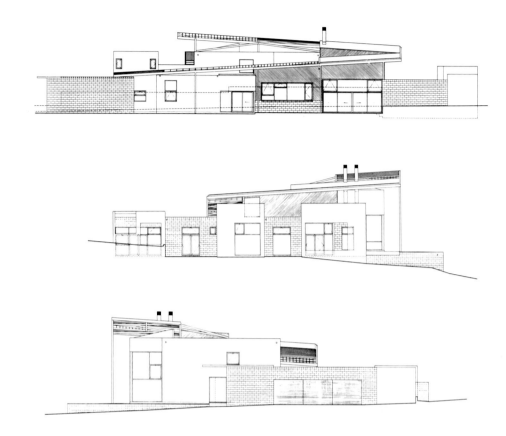

rear (west) elevation; south elevation; north elevation

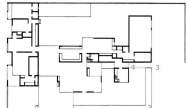

1 east facade (preceding pages) **2,3** entry: trellis, reflecting pool **4** pivoting entry door, guestrooms to

5 under library, bar and reception **6** stairway to library **7** view from library stair

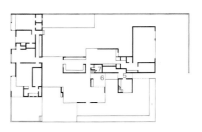

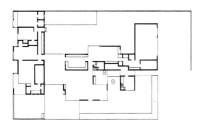

8 view back toward entry with sculpture garden at right **9** view from sculpture garden

10 living room toward entry and library loft **11** sketch of dining room toward kitchen, living room, and library loft

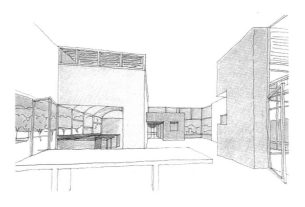

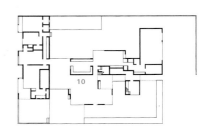

12 living room toward sculpture garden and Reno beyond, with Donald Judd boxes on wall **13** corner window, northeast view

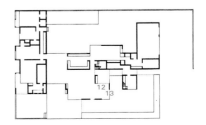

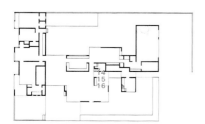

14 library loft toward living room **15, 16** details of library loft

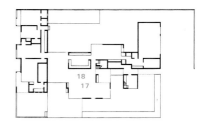

17 dining room from living room **18** dining room (table by Terry Hunziker)

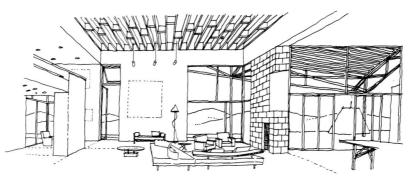

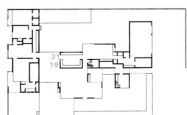

19 living room from dining room **20** sketch of living room **21** view of valley from dining room

22 dining-room terrace at night **23** view from southeast **24** early sketch of east elevation

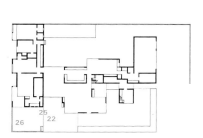

25 detail of bathroom cube and trellis **26** dining-room terrace, view toward living room with bathroom cube in foreground

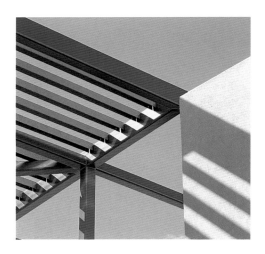

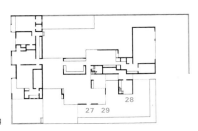

27 trellis and stucco outside living room **28** detail of trellis **29** view past living room to guest wing

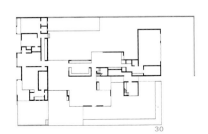

30 view from northeast, guest wing in foreground **31** night view

30

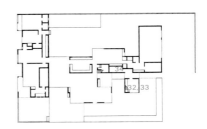

32, 33 guest-wing stair to bedroom and bath **34** powder room with custom sink

35 dining-room terrace, view toward south **36** sunroom with stucco trellis over bedroom **37** detail of stucco trellis

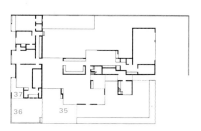

38

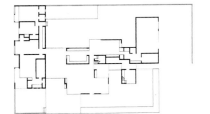

39

38 west and south facades **39** south facade with stucco sunroom trellises in front of bedrooms

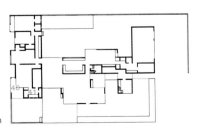

40 view to south from sunroom outside master bedroom **41** master bath toward master bedroom

42 view into backyard from kitchen **43** kitchen toward dining room

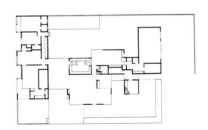

44 kitchen toward family room **45** detail of kitchen cabinet

46 interior wood trellis in family room 47 family room with kitchen to the left

48 family-room aviary **49** original sketch of family room **50** backyard with view to kitchen and family room

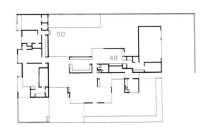

51 pool with view to west **52** sketch of backyard **53** trellis rising to south **54** detail of stucco/cement block and trellis

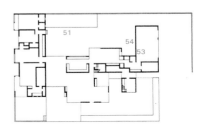

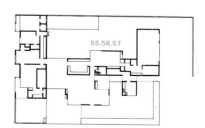

55, 56, 57 kitchen/family room trellis and details

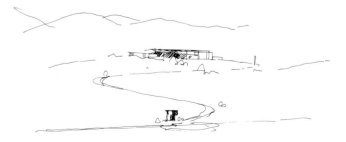

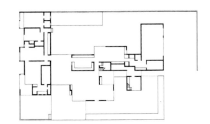

58

58 view from west: house cut into hill **59** sketch with future guest house and gate

Afterword I have been asked to discuss the house Mark Mack designed from the point of view of the client—and
Peter Stremmel after experiencing the phenomenon of living in it for a full year. Turkey and I thought we knew this
house intimately, having spent a year with Mark on the design process, then visiting the site daily for
over a year and a half during construction. But we did not realize the profound effect the space
would have on us after the passage of four extreme seasons on this arid hilltop. Almost one thou-
sand feet higher than the city of Reno (at 4,400 feet), we overlook it to the east and have a com-
manding, almost overwhelming view of the Sierras to the west.

Our primary requirement of Mark was that he design spaces that could be extremely versatile for a
changing showcase of contemporary artworks, yet still be comfortable as living areas. The character
of the spaces changes dramatically depending on the season. In the late spring, summer, and early
fall, the house and its various patios and enclosures become an extension of the exterior, whereas, in
winter, the dramatic interior spaces are the primary focus. We have also found that the light changes
constantly, creating fascinating patterns on the exterior walls from the vertical supports and horizon-
tal slats of the trellis. Great care was taken to avoid direct sunlight on the main walls, which display
large works of contemporary art. This flexibility was Mark's design philosophy throughout.

As visitors enter through the pivoting front door, they immediately pass the guest room/loft and
encounter a passageway with a wall of floor-to-ceiling glass which looks onto a semienclosed outdoor sculpture area. The living and dining rooms are spacious, with high ceilings. Combining comfort
and formality with a variety of interesting surfaces and textures, they provide an ideal venue for modern and contemporary art. The interior furnishings and accessories were by Seattle-based designer
Terry Hunziker, who was sensitive to avoid contemporary clichés; he created elegant, restrained
seating areas somewhat influenced by the designs of Jean-Michel Frank.

The overall plan is deceptively simple, but every wall, window, and door relate to some other wall,
line, or plane in the house. This design organization is not immediately apparent, but gives a subcon-
scious sense of harmony throughout. The exterior shapes, forms, textures and colors create a dramatic morphology. Ironically, however, these forms are not particularly complex, nor does the house
feel radical within the vernacular of contemporary architecture. Rather, it is an exhilarating and
dynamic structure that answers, for Turkey and me, questions of who we are and how we deal with
our constantly changing and stimulating environment.